MW00532927

First Edition: August 2019

McCulloch, Ryan.

Guitarchitecture - A Creative Approach to Learning the Guitar / Ryan McCulloch. – 1st Ed.

ISBN-13: 978-1-7343611-0-0

 https://www.facebook.com/NextGenMusicSessions/

 YouTube: Next Generation Music Sessions

Page Intentionally Left Blank

Table of Contents

Acknowledgements

Like many good ideas, this book was a collaboration with many different brilliant minds and inspiring individuals. I would first like to thank Tim and Rachel McCulloch for their incessant support and encouragement, I still carry many of the lessons and gifts you have given me to this day.

Alex Johnson, whose keen intellect inspired many of these pages, showed me that wit, patience, and humor are the most effective in one's pedagogical toolkit as technique and experience.

I would like to thank Karen King, who has never failed to point out how much empathy and active listening can really pave the way to long-lasting connections.

Thanks Madeline Thiry for making comments and suggestions at such an early stage.

To my coworkers, Brenden and Garrison, you never cease to inspire me and I hope that we will continue this great journey of ours for decades.

Julie Cox, you have always believed in me and been so thoughtfully supportive.

To Erin McCulloch and Julia Thompson, thank you for putting up with countless years of practice and being so inspiring all the while.

To Jennifer Kagan, thanks for making this dream a reality.

Finally, I want to thank my wife Tricia McCulloch and daughter Layla McCulloch for putting up with my absence and being such guiding forces in my presence—this book would not have been possible without your warmth.

Introduction

The purpose of *Guitarchitecture* is to provide the novice guitarist with simple visualization tools to map out the notes on the guitar neck and provide the novice guitarist a basic music theory foundation.

In essence, this is a basic music theory book in that theory pedagogy begins with intervals, but the method here is in line with the development of guitar technique in the twentieth century as well. Virtuosic guitar playing has been transformed by guitarists that largely cannot read traditional music, yet the music is often anything but simple. For this and other reasons, this book uses neck diagrams and tablature as opposed to traditional notation.

The book is divided into six chapters.
Each chapter focuses on one interval.

Located at the end of each chapter are several recommended written and performance exercises. Each chapter is accompanied with three etudes ranging in difficulty from easiest to hardest and a few duets. The etudes and duets reinforce the interval that was covered in the chapter and reinforces the material in a short, yet musical way.

Should the guitarist have no experience with rhythmic or slash notation, there are four pages of picking exercises in Appendix A (page 39) that will help the guitarist to read rhythmic notation, develop a musical intuition for alternate picking, and help them develop the ability to play in time. Additionally, all of the etudes incorporate legato techniques (slides, hammer-ons, and pull-offs).

There are a few articulation exercises in Appendix B (page 44). Every musical example, etude, duet, and exercise should be performed with a metronome, even if it is at a slow tempo. Habitually practicing with a metronome will significantly enhance the novice's fluency on the guitar.

I use this book in tandem with other pedagogical methodologies in my studio. For this reason, the exercises are short, but they are designed to be challenging for the novice. This method will help prepare the novice for more challenging literature and is broad enough so that it can be used for various types of students from aspiring professional musicians to those in other professions who use the guitar as a vehicle for relaxation.

While this book could be used for self-study, it was intended to be used with a knowledgeable expert to help guide the novice.

1 | The Music Alphabet

In music we use letters to refer to all the available notes in Western music. These letters come from our alphabet, but we only use the first seven letters. We will begin by looking at letters **A** through **G** in the music alphabet:

A * B C * D * E F * G

Questions? Any questions? Surely you have noticed the asterisks between some of the letters. The asterisks are placed between some of the letters because the distance between each letter is very important. In music we use the word interval to describe the distance between two notes.

For instance, **B** to **C** is what we call a *minor second*, or what most musicians call a half step (a minor second and a half step are synonyms or words meaning the same thing).

> *A half step is equivalent to*
> *one fret on the guitar.*

B to C is spaced more closely above to indicate they are located right next to one another, or more specifically they are a minor 2nd apart. Play up the music alphabet half-steps on your E-string (open E and the 1st fret (F), and the 7th fret (B) to the 8th fret (C)).

Another type of interval occurs between **A** to **B**. This interval is called a *major second* and is also known as a whole step.

> *The major second is equivalent*
> *to two frets on the guitar.*

Why do some notes have whole–step distances and the others have half–step distances?

In Western music there are actually twelve different notes, so the entire music alphabet looks like this:

A A#/Bb B C C#/Db D D#/Eb E F F#/Gb G G#/Ab

This is fairly confusing, so for now just remember some notes have whole steps and others have half steps. Why? **B**ecause **C**ats **E**at **F**ish. What note comes after **G**? **A**, you just start back at the beginning of the music alphabet.

What are the string names on your guitar?

Eddie Ate Dynamite Good Bye Eddie

Suggested Assignments

① The student should play their open strings and repeat the names of each string after playing each string.

Use each of the open strings to identify whole-step and half-step intervals between the open string and the first alphabet note on the string.

② Have them write out the answers to the following problems.
Name the interval and number of frets between:

    a.   D up to E

    b.   B up to C

    c.   F up to G

    d.   B up to A

    e.   C up to B

    f.   F up to E

③ Define an interval.

④ Have the student memorize the natural (alphabet) note names between the first to the third frets on the E, A, and D strings.

⑤ Have the student play up and back down the low E and A strings (fingering is not important).

Second Exercises

Etudes: All etudes in this book should be performed with a metronome. Begin at quarter note = 60. Progressively increase the tempo up to quarter note = 120. Below each etude and duet are suggested fingerings (these are the fingerings that I use). Do not move on to the next etude until the assigned etude has been performed at 120 beats per minute. The second etudes are divided into **E**-string etudes (**A** - **C**) and **A**-string etudes (**A** - **C**).

(A) E-string Second Etude A

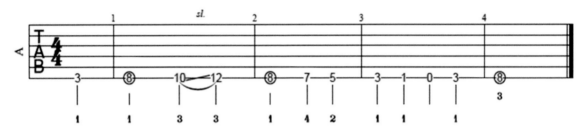

(B) E-string Second Etude B

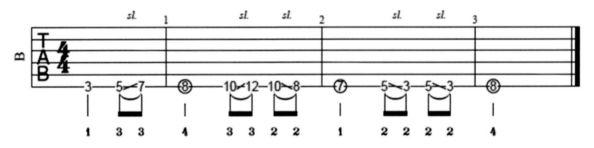

(C) E-string Second Etude

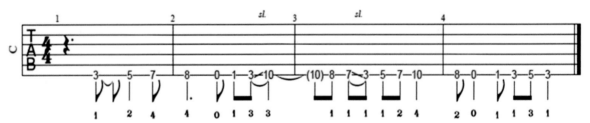

Etudes: All etudes in this book should be performed with a metronome. Begin at quarter note = 60. Progressively increase the tempo up to quarter note = 120. Below each etude and duet are suggested fingerings (these are the fingerings that I use). Do not move on to the next etude until the assigned etude has been performed at 120 beats per minute. The second etudes are divided into E-string etudes (**A - C**) and A-string etudes (**A - C**).

Ⓐ   A-string Second Etude A

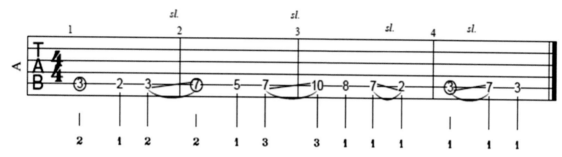

Ⓑ   A-string Second Etude B

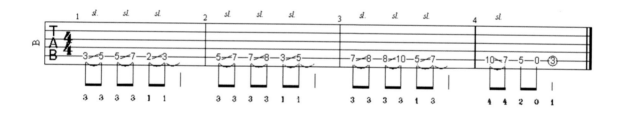

Ⓒ   A-string Second Etude C

This Page Intentionally Left Blank

2 | The Perfect Fourth

Now that you have a decent grasp on the musical alphabet, I will move on to the concept of "shape" on the guitar. In the last chapter, I introduced the term interval, and said that intervals were either one or two frets (minor or major seconds) within the music alphabet. In the next few chapters I will introduce a few other types of intervals. While these intervals are pretty easy to understand, their application will take some time. Be patient with yourself and with your teacher—you can learn this!

I will start this chapter by defining a new term: *shape*. A shape is a finger pattern that can be performed with any combination of fingers. The first three intervals you will learn in this chapter will be shapes played on adjacent strings (strings next to one another). Work on playing each of these intervals with any finger combination.

Let's begin with the low **E** string. What is the interval between the **E** and **A** strings? Begin with the **E** string and count up to **A** with the music alphabet. **E = 1, F = 2, G = 3, A = 4**; therefore, it is a fourth. Go through the following adjacent string pairs:

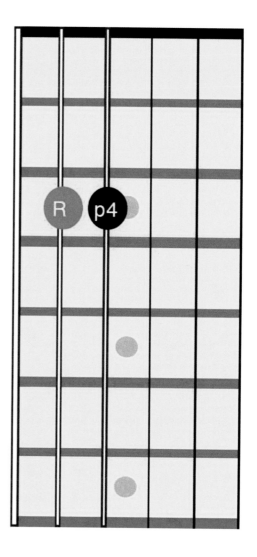

A to D

D to G

B to E

These string pairs make up String Set 1. What fret numbers do you play when playing the **E** to **A** strings? Are they the same or different? Because they are the same, I can make a simple rule about this interval: Any String Set 1 pair will have the same intervallic relationships. Meaning, whenever you put your fingers down on the same frets on adjacent strings on string set 1, you are playing a fourth. For example, play the third frets on the **A** and **D** strings—this is a fourth.

The *perfect fourth*, for now, will always have this shape. We will refer to the bottom note in any of these intervals as the bass note and the note that lies a fourth above the bass note is called the fourth. In the diagram on page 13, the note labelled "R" is the bass note. Which note is that in the music alphabet? Then if you know that note, which note is a perfect fourth, or a fourth, above the bass note?

If the notes in the music alphabet are arranged in fourths, then only one fourth DOES NOT look like *(and more importantly, sound like)* the others. In order to understand the difference, we should carefully define the E–A fourth.

E – A contains two major seconds (F – G, G – A) and one minor second (E – F). We call this fourth a perfect fourth (P4). Go back and think through the other fourths. Do they each have two major seconds plus one minor second?

Now let's consider F – B. This interval contains three major seconds (F – G, G – A, A – B). This interval is called an *augmented fourth* (A4).[1] It is important to remember that all fourths are perfect except: F – B.

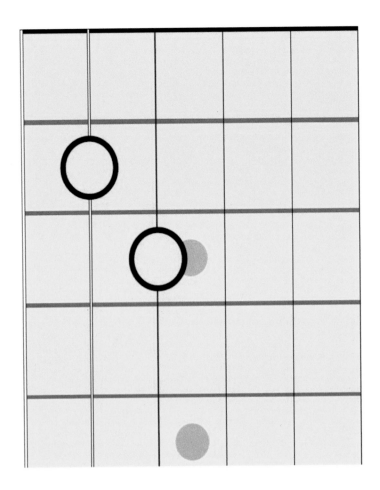

[1] It is also often called a tritone, but for our purposes, we will use the term augmented fourth because it is more specific.

Written and Performance Work

1   What is a shape?

2   What does adjacent mean?

3   True or False: You should always play the bass note with your first finger?

4   Practice and perform the fourth etudes.

5   Practice and perform the fourth duets.

While these tasks may seem tedious, their purpose is to make intervals and notes very familiar to you. Think about this, how often do you have to diagram every sentence you speak?

How often do you think to yourself:

"Well, *I* is the subject, *hate* is the verb, and *these exercises* is the object."
(Some of you might have added in the adjective *stupid* as well.)

You don't do this because you know these and other words so well that thinking about how they work in a sentence is second nature to you.

⚙️④ Fourth Etudes & Duets

Etudes: Students should be able to perform at least two of the three etudes before attempting the duets. Be able to identify all the fourths in the three etudes and two duets.

Ⓐ Write all of the note names below each note in this etude. Focus on playing the rhythms properly. Every single note in this etude will be a downstroke. Write the note names under the etude and memorize them. Finally, make sure the slides in measures one and three do not alter the rhythms at all.

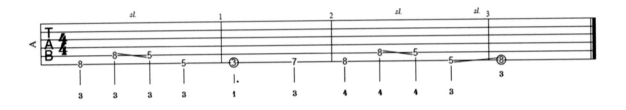

Ⓑ This etude incorporates all three legato articulations with an eighth-note pick up and eighth-note motives. I recommend shifting into and out of positions in measures one through three with the first finger. Write the note names under the etude and memorize them.

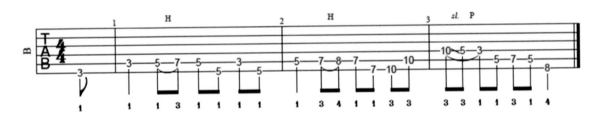

Ⓒ This is the most difficult etude of the three. It makes use of all three types of basic-legato articulations, it requires the guitarist to be comfortable with syncopation (extended emphasis on the up beats or "ands"), and therefore, requires the guitarist to perform multiple upstrokes in succession.

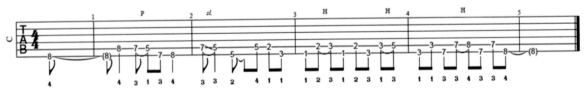

 Duets

Duets: Each duet is to be performed by two guitarists with a metronome between 60 and 120 beats per minute. Guitarists should take turns performing both parts. In the first etude, guitar 1 performs a melody while guitar 2 performs an accompaniment. The accompaniment is made of "sus chords" or chords with a root, fourth and fifth.

These chords are quintessential in contemporary music in many genres. Study how the melody reinforces the harmony. In the second etude, guitar 1 and 2 perform an imitative melody that requires both players to perform closely in eighth notes. Each player should continuously subdivide eighth notes even when they are resting.

Duet ❶:

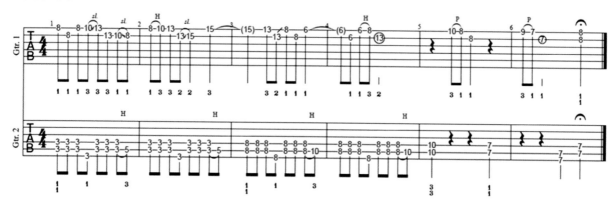

Duet ❷:

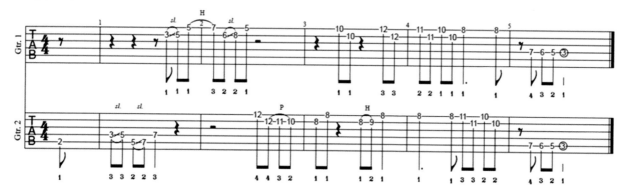

This page intentionally left blank.

3 | The Major Third

The good news is that after you are familiar with the perfect fourth you will be able to play the most frequently used intervals used to make chords and melodies. This chapter explores the major third.

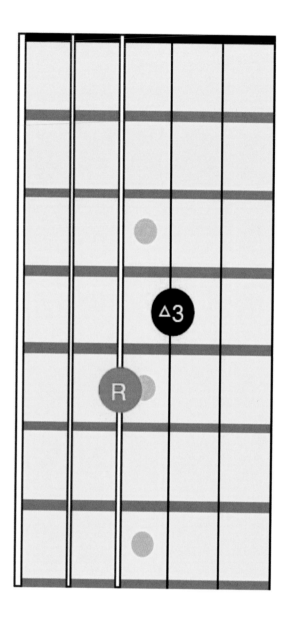

The major third is a half–step below the perfect fourth provided the same bass note is used for both intervals.

On the adjacent string pairs **E – A, A – D, D – G, B – E**, the major third will always have this shape.

The major third can also be found on the same string as the bass note, and is sometimes played this way as well. If the bass note **G** is played (third fret on the E-string), then the major third on the same string will be the **B** on the seventh fret.

How many whole steps, or major seconds are in this interval? This interval is shown in the diagram to the right.

If the bass note and the third are played in succession (one right after the other), then the interval is called a *melodic interval*. In this case, it will be a melodic third. If the bass note and third are played simultaneously (at the same time), then the interval is called a *harmonic interval*.

As you might have guessed, melodic intervals are used for melodies and harmonic intervals are used for harmonies or chords. Though these distinctions are not mutually exclusive, some melodies use harmonic intervals and some chords make use of melodic intervals. This might seem confusing now, but once you can play these intervals and etudes fluidly, then you will see that really harmonic and melodic intervals are really two sides of the same coin.

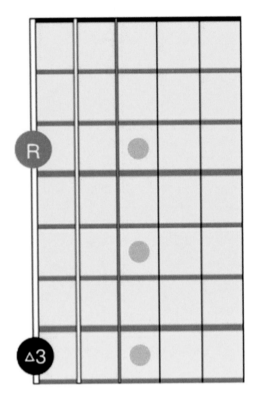

The final thing to think about, before moving on to the major third exercises is: how many major thirds are in the music alphabet? If you understand that every major third has two major seconds (or two whole-steps) then we can figure this problem out. Notice that skipping every other note in the music alphabet gives us two types of intervals: one with two whole-steps and one with a step-and-a-half. We will ignore this last interval for the moment and focus on the major third. Notice:

$$A - C = 1 \text{ step} + \tfrac{1}{2}; \quad B - D = \tfrac{1}{2} + 1 \text{ step}; \quad \text{but } C - E = 2 \text{ steps}$$

What are the other two major thirds in the music alphabet? **F – A** and **G – B**.

Written and Performance Work

❶ What are the three major thirds in the music alphabet?
   a. Write them out here:
   b. Play them on your **E** and **A** strings.

❷ Practice and perform the major Third etudes.

❸ Practice and perform the major Third duets.

⚙️③ Major Third Exercises

Ⓐ Write the note names below each note in this etude.
One of these notes is not in the key of **C**. Mark a star above the note that does not belong to **C** major. Measures one and two imply a **C** major chord, why? Measure three implies a **D** major chord, why? Measure four implies a **G7** chord, why?

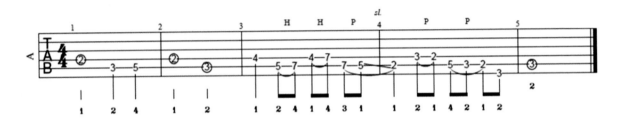

Ⓑ Write the note names below each note in this etude.
Etude **B** outlines **C** major, **A7**, **D7**, and **G7** chords. Play these chords before attempting to play the etude so you can hear how they sound with the melody. Notice how the melody outlines major thirds over each of these chords.

Ⓒ Write the note names below each note in this etude.
Etude **C** outlines the chords **A – C – D7 – E7 – G7 – A**. This type of chord progression occurs in many types of music. Notice how the melody outlines major thirds with syncopation.

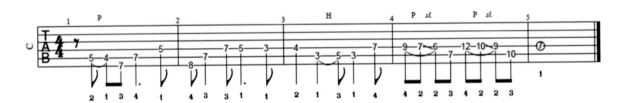

Duet ❶:

This is the first etude in 6/8. Each measure contains six beats, but unlike 4/4 in which the quarter note equals one beat, the eighth note equals one beat. Furthermore, in 6/8 there are accents on beats one and four. Practice counting to a metronome: (**1** 2 3, **4** 5 6) several times before studying this duet.

Finally, this duet makes use of the whole-tone scale with some chromatic notes. A whole tone scale is a symmetrical scale made entirely of whole tones. The whole-tone scale beginning on C is:
C – D – E – F# – G# – A# – C. Which notes in this duet lie outside of the C whole-tone scale? How many major thirds are there in this scale?

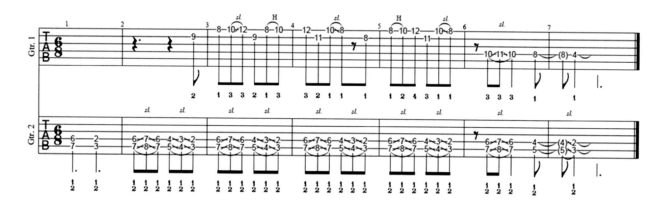

Duet ❷:

Major thirds can be used to imply the three major chords of C major (the three major chords of any key really). What are the three major chords in C major? Where do you hear these chords in this duet?

This page intentionally left blank.

4 | The Minor Third

Similar to the major third, the minor third can be played as a harmonic interval or a melodic interval on the guitar. Unlike the major third, the minor third is performed just as frequently either on adjacent strings or on the same string.

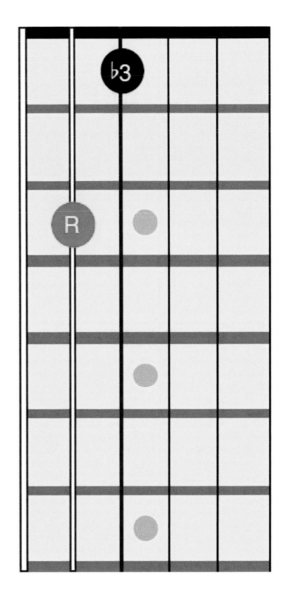

If the minor third is played on an adjacent string, then it can be found just a half-step below the Major third.

Play the **C** on your **A**-string (third fret), and find your major third. If you lower your major third one half-step, then your finger shape should look like this →

This minor third can be either a melodic or a harmonic interval since both these notes are on adjacent strings and they can be played simultaneously or in succession.

As mentioned above, the minor third is often played on the same string. This minor third will only ever be a melodic interval. Start with your first finger on the bass note **C** (on the **A**–string) and play up three frets with your fourth finger. Note that the fourth finger normally plays this fret if each finger is designated to the given fret below it. In the music alphabet, minor thirds occur between:
D – F, E – G, A – C, B – D.

*As you can see,
the minor third contains
one major second and
one minor second.*

Playing the music alphabet in thirds is a quintessential skill because it improves your technique (dexterity, right and left–hand coordination), and it is also an essential pattern that you will hear in many types of music. Just like the Major third, the minor third can be played both as a melodic and harmonic interval.

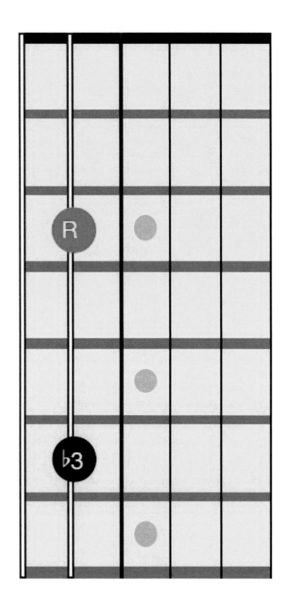

Written and Performance Work

① Play the music alphabet in thirds on adjacent strings in harmonic intervals. Practice these thirds on the **E – A; A – D; D – G;** and **B – E** strings.

② Play the music alphabet in thirds on adjacent strings in melodic intervals. Begin with a strict pattern (on the **E – A** strings respectively) and play **F – A; G – B,** etc. This forces you to always begin with the bass note and follow it with the third. Do the same for the **A – D** strings and the **D – G** strings.

③ Play the music alphabet in thirds on adjacent strings in melodic intervals. Reverse the previous pattern so that you are playing the third and then the bass note.

④ Now play the pattern alternating. For instance, begin with the **E – A** strings. Play **G – B** and then play **C** (on the **A**–string) down to **A.** Continue this pattern so that you play ascending and descending thirds.

⑤ Reverse the pattern above so that you are playing descending and ascending intervals.

⑥ Practice and perform the third etudes.

⑦ Practice and perform the third duets.

A Write the note names below each note in this etude.

Etude **A** is in **A** minor and makes use of the **A** harmonic minor scale (A – B – C – D – E – F – G# – A). Notice the repetition of the initial descending minor third melodic pattern in the second measure. Repetition is a common and powerful melodic device. The pattern is then repeated down a step in the scale.

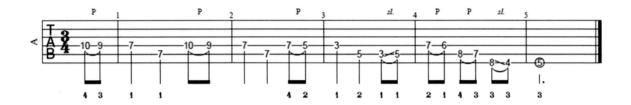

B Write the note names below each note in this etude.

Etude **B** is in **C** minor and begins with a minor third (C – Eb). Measure six makes use of the blue-note in **C** (F#) and ends with two different **C** minor scales (measure 7). Be careful with your fingering on this etude.

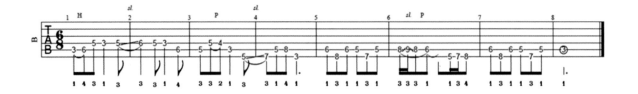

C Write the note names below each note in this etude.

Etude **C** opens with a minor third (D – F descending). Enjoy the syncopation and the legato in measures three and four.

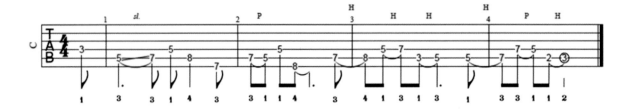

Duets

Duet ❶:

Write the note names below each note in this duet. Duet #1 makes use of diatonic thirds (thirds from the scale), and therefore not every third is minor. Identify which thirds are minor in this duet.

This duet makes use of palm muting (P.M.) and open strings (let ring) in both parts. The relationship between the two parts is what is referred to as imitation, in which, one part nearly copies the other.

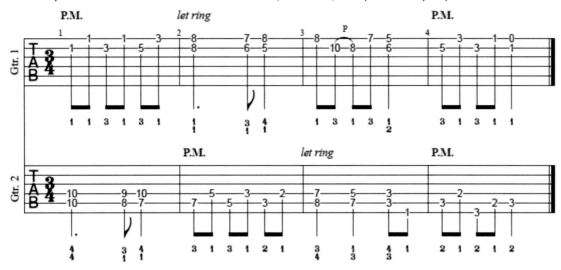

Duet ❷:

Write the note names below each note in this duet. Duet #2 is in **A** minor and each part begins by quickly imitating the next on each beat. The guitarists need to subdivide eighths really well in order to play this short duet.

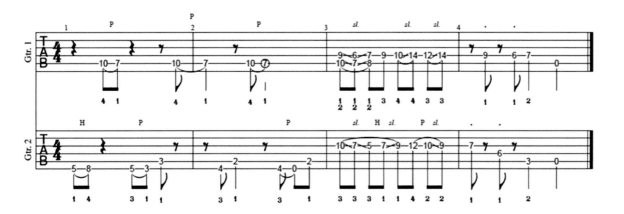

This page intentionally left blank.

5 | The Perfect Fifth and Diminished Fifth

The next interval we will learn and work in this book is the *perfect fifth*. Assume that you have a given bass note "C" (third fret on the A-string). The perfect fourth above the C, as you well know by now, is F. The perfect fifth is just a whole step above the fourth. This interval is more commonly known as a "power chord" in most guitar literature.

The perfect fifth (P5)
lies a whole-step above
the fourth and has
3 whole steps plus 1 half step.

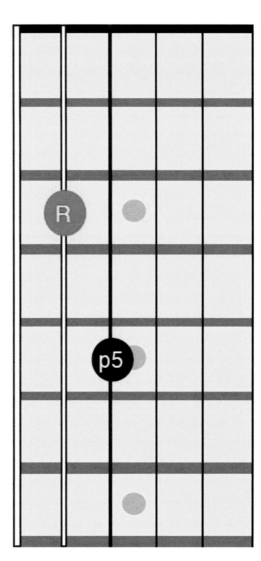

All of the **P5**s in the music alphabet are perfect except for **B – F**. This is a diminished fifth (d5), which means the fifth is smaller than perfect (3 whole steps). But you have already encountered this interval. It is the exact same shape as the augmented fourth or a tritone.

This brings up the last theoretical topic we will use in this book before we turn to studying scales and repertoire: inversion. Inversion seems to be confusing, but does not have to be. Think about what the word "invert" means: to put upside down or in the opposite order.

So, if the interval F – B is an augmented fourth (F = 1; G = 2; A = 3; B = 4), and if we flip these notes around we get B – F (B = 1; C = 2; D = 3; E = 4; F = 5) or a diminished fifth.

What this relationship expresses is a rule one can use to find the inversion of any interval. Notice we are just using two notes, right? F – B. In fact, what we are really doing is using three notes: F – B – F.

F	B	F
A4	**d5**	**= 9 (4+5)**

Written and Performance Work

1 Play all **P5**s in the key of **C** major on the **E**, **A**, **D**, and **B** strings. Focus most of your attention on memorizing the **P5**s on the **E** and **A**-strings.

　　a.　Play the intervals as harmonic and melodic intervals.

2 Practice and perform the fifth etudes and the fifth duets.

Fifth Exercises

Etudes:

A   Write the note names below each note in this etude.

Etude A is a melody that outlines the descending fifth progression in **G** major (**G** – **C** – **D/F#** – **G/B** – **Em** – **Am** – **D7** – **G**). Fifths will often be used to add color to common chords you already know. For example, the last chord in measure eight is a **G** chord with a 6 (**E** on the second fret of the **D**-string) and an add 9 (the open **A**-string).

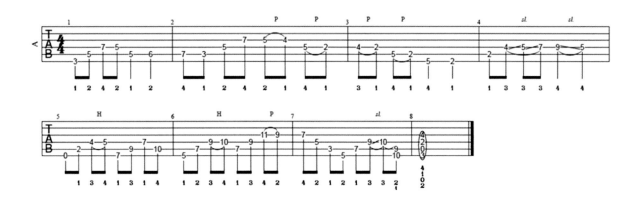

B   Write the note names below each note in this etude.

Etude **B** uses melodically and harmonically over a droned **E**-bass note.

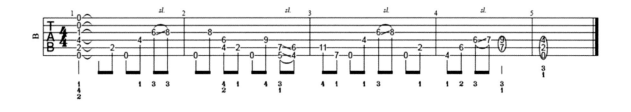

C   Write the note names below each note in this etude.

Etude **C** begins in **C** but by measure 2, with the **Bb** on beat two, modulates to **F**. It is only in the very last bar that we hear **C** major again because of the tritone (diminished fifth/augmented fourth) **F** – **B**. The tritone resolves to **E** – **C** respectively.

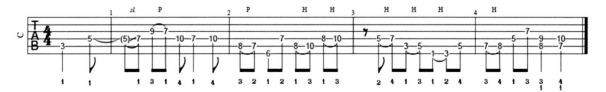

 Duets

Duet ❶:

Write the note names below each note in this duet.
Duet #1 illustrates several common uses of the fifth. First, guitar 1 performs fifths as power chords (mostly) in a descending fifth progression in **G** major. Be sure to employ both palm muting (P.M.) and open string (let ring) techniques with the right hand. Guitar 2 articulates fifths alternating with thirds throughout most of the melody.

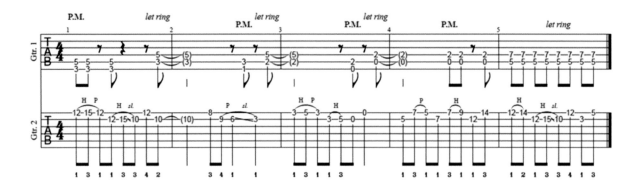

Duet ❷:

Write the note names below each note in this duet. Duet #2 fuses traditional uses of the fifth with a non-traditional sequence. While guitar 1 plays a common **G** minor pentatonic progression in power chords, guitar 2 plays a two measure descending line that colors the power chords much more than each root and fifth imply.

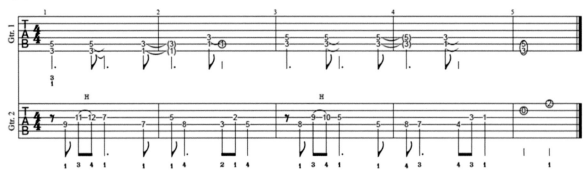

6 | The Octave

The final interval this book covers is the octave. From a very practical perspective, this interval is really quite simple both physically and conceptually. Conceptually an octave means that if your bass note is a "C," then the octave is a "C" above the bass note. If your bass note is an "E," then the octave is an "E." In each of these examples we are counting eight notes. See below:

$$C = 1; D = 2; E = 3; F = 4; G = 5; A = 6; B = 7; C = 8;$$
$$\text{or } C\text{---}{>}C = \text{an octave}$$

The initial C and the final C are an octave apart from one another (8 notes). When playing octaves, you will notice it is difficult to hear the difference between the pitches. Try singing the different notes and the difference in pitch becomes very clear. On the guitar, the octave looks very similar to the fifth (though the octave should not be mistaken for the fifth!).

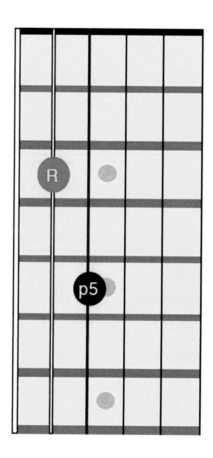 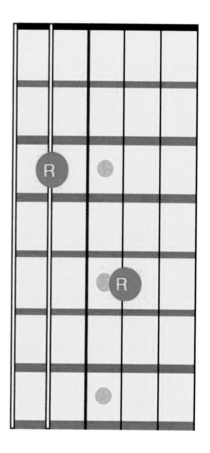

Despite the fact that this interval is easy to play and think about, I have saved the octave for the final chapter for two reasons. First, because all of the intervals (and their corresponding shapes) presented in this book have been intervals either on the adjacent or same strings. This interval, however, skips one string (notice the string in between). This means that muting the string adjacent to the bass note is mandatory.

Second, the octave allows you to see inversionally-related intervals, and therefore, all of the previous intervals need to be memorized. The term *invert* means to put upside down or in the opposite position. Being able to see the octave and knowing the inverse interval by way of the octave will allow you to learn the neck of the guitar thoroughly. Let's look at an example.

Assume your bass note is **G** (the third fret on the **E**-string). The **G** one octave above this bass note lies on the fifth fret on the **D**-string. Having "octavision" allows you to quickly and easily identify notes on the guitar with which you may be less familiar. Assume that you take that same bass note, **G**, but now you reference the pitch on the fourth fret of the **D**-string instead.

Notice that in every example in this book is counted up from a reference pitch. Intervals are, for our purposes, only ever measured by counting forward through the alphabet. It is easy to see with octavision that this pitch is an **F#**. If you reference the bass note **G** (the fourth fret on the **D**-string), and measure up to the **F#**, then you get a major seventh.

*A major seventh is a minor second below
the octave and a minor seventh is a
major second below the octave.*

By its very definition the major seventh is the inversion of the minor second (meaning the major seventh is measure down from the octave and not up from the bass note). This is inversion. Inversion helps you see intervals larger than a perfect fifth.

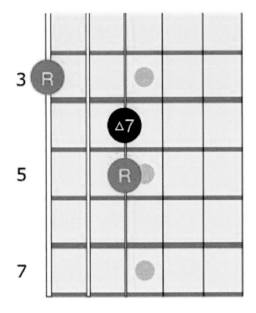

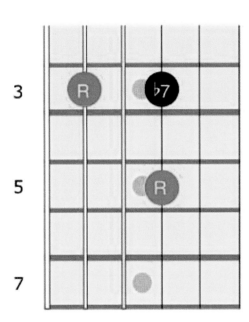

Inversion provides insights into major and minor sixths as well.

A major sixth is a minor third below the octave.
The minor sixth is either a minor third below the
octave or a minor second above the perfect fifth.

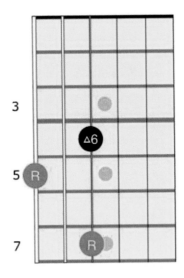 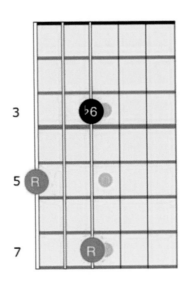 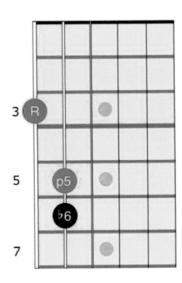

Luckily, I have a method for quickly memorizing inversions. All intervals and their inversions sum to 9. The quality changes to its opposite (so a major interval inverts to a minor and vice versa). See the chart below for details:

$$m2 \longrightarrow M7$$

$$M2 \longrightarrow m7$$

$$m3 \longrightarrow M6$$

$$M3 \longrightarrow m6$$

$$P4 \longrightarrow P5 \text{ (and vice versa)}$$

Written and Performance Work

1 The student should set a metronome and play a **C** major scale on the **G**-string. Begin by referencing the octave **C**, the fifth fret. Do the same exercise on the **D**-string.

2 Write the major and minor sevenths in **C** major.
   a. major sevenths:
   b. minor sevenths:

3 Write the major and minor sixths in **C** major.
   a. major sevenths:
   b. minor sevenths:

4 Now that the student knows what all of the interval shapes look like, they should start playing scales in intervals. Begin with seconds, then move to thirds and then sixths.

Review Exercises

Instructions:

These diagrams are intended to help the student identify the intervals covered in *Guitarchitecture*. The student can label the intervals inside these very common chord and scale shapes. For the time being ignore the intervals on the G – B strings.

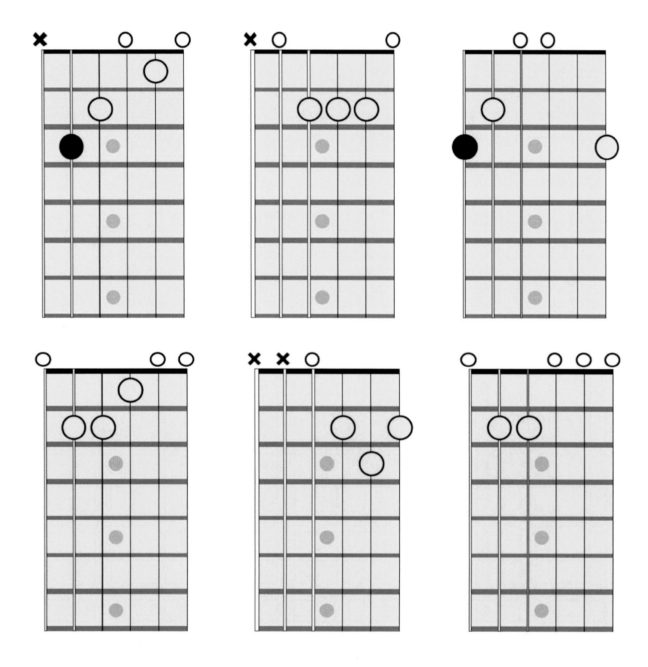

Review Exercises *(Continued)*

Instructions: These diagrams are intended to help the student identify the intervals covered in *Guitarchitecture*. The student can label the intervals inside these very common chord and scale shapes. For the time being ignore the intervals on the **G** – **B** strings.

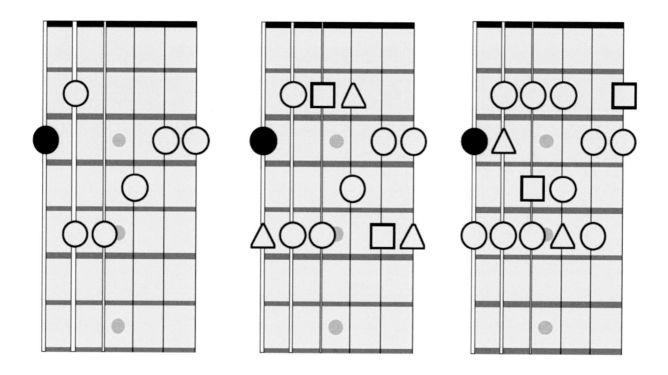

This page left intentionally blank.

Appendix A | Picking Exercises

The following picking exercises are designed to help novice guitarists practice reading rhythmic notation. Since all of the etudes and duets use rhythmic notation, a firm grasp of the specifics of rhythm and picking is mandatory. First, all durations longer than a quarter note (whole, half, dotted-half, etc.) are to be played with a downstroke only.

When the eighth note rhythm is introduced on the first sheet, the downbeats (beats 1 – 4) should be a downstroke and the upbeats should be played with an upstroke. When the eighth-note rest is introduced on the second sheet the single eighth-note on the upbeat will always be played with an upstroke.

Notes

Each exercise is to be performed on either the third, fifth or seventh frets of either the E or A-string.

One note is to be performed for each exercise.

Play each exercise with a metronome beginning at 50 beats per minute up to 120 beats per minute.

Do not move on to the next set of exercises until the entire page has been performed without error at 120 beats per minute.

Appendix A | Picking Exercise 1

Appendix A | Picking Exercise 2

Appendix A | Picking Exercise3: Syncopation

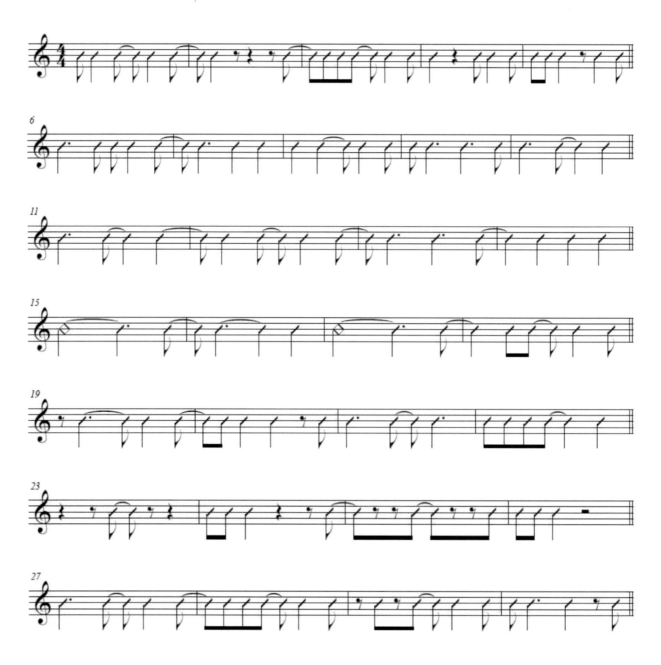

Appendix A | Picking Exercise 4: Sixteenth-note Patterns

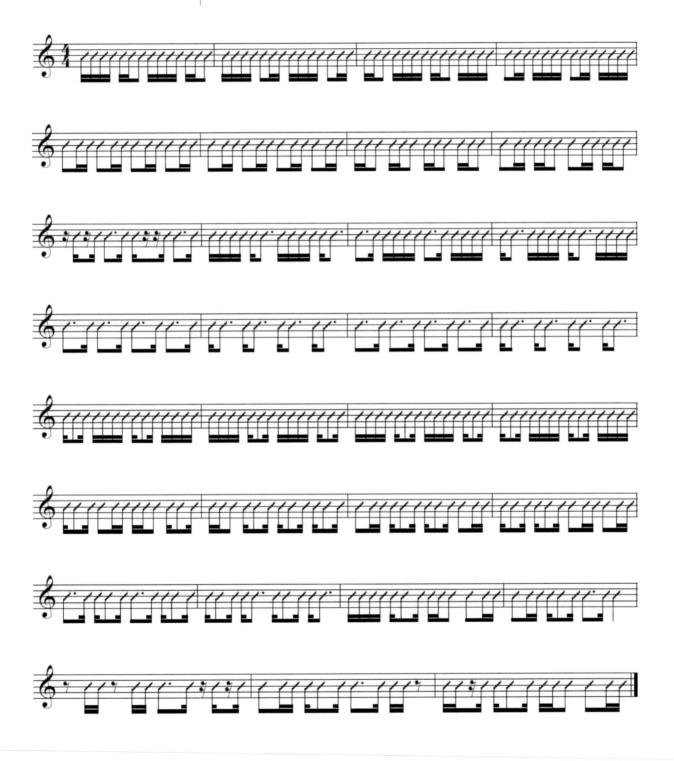

Appendix B | Articulation Exercises

Directions: The exercises in this appendix are intended to help novice guitarists develop their legato technique. These exercises are divided into hammer-ons (**A-E**) and pull-offs (**F-J**). Each exercise is one measure long, but should be repeated three times (played for a total of four measures). A measure of rest should follow the four measures and then the exercise should be repeated until it is comfortable at the given speed. Practice each of these exercises from quarter equals 40 up to 120.

❶ **Hammer-on Exercise A**

❷ **Hammer-on Exercise B**

❸ **Hammer-on Exercise C**

❹ **Hammer-on Exercise D**

❺ **Hammer-on Exercise E**

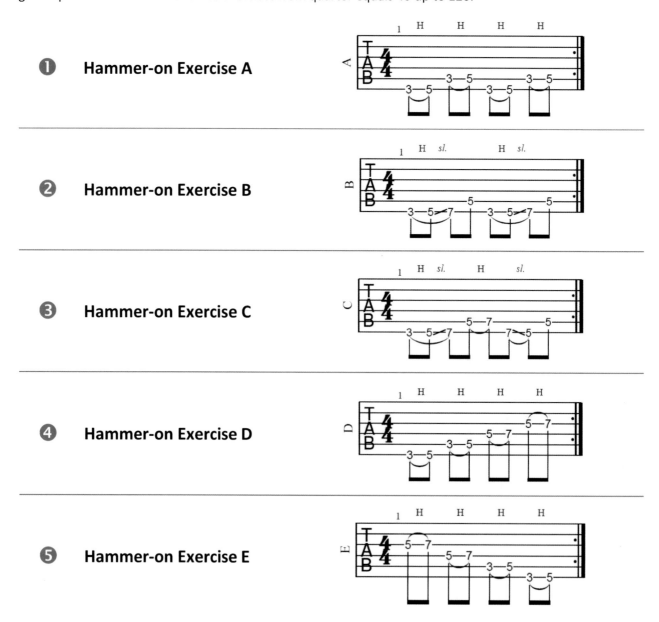

Appendix B | Articulation Exercises *(Continued)*

Directions: The exercises in this appendix are intended to help novice guitarists develop their legato technique. These exercises are divided into hammer-ons (**A-E**) and pull-offs (**F-J**). Each exercise is one measure long, but should be repeated three times (played for a total of four measures).
A measure of rest should follow the four measures and then the exercise should be repeated until it is comfortable at the given speed. Practice each of these exercises from quarter equals 40 up to 120.

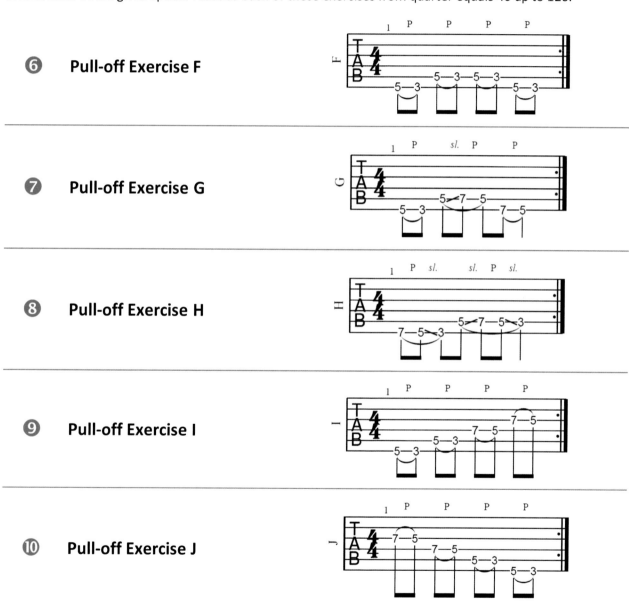

⑥ **Pull-off Exercise F**

⑦ **Pull-off Exercise G**

⑧ **Pull-off Exercise H**

⑨ **Pull-off Exercise I**

⑩ **Pull-off Exercise J**

Appendix C | Attributions

Cover, Back Cover	Parchment Paper Background Graphic https://www.freepik.com/free-photos-vectors/vintage Vintage photo created by rawpixel.com - www.freepik.com</a> Guitar Photo Credit: Insert Name Here Font: Handwriting Draft Font https://www.dafont.com/handwriting-draft.font http://fonts-lab.com
Icons on Copyright Page, Table of Contents Page, Pages 5-7, 11-13, 17-19, 23-25, 28-30, 35-37	Icons made by https://www.flaticon.com/authors/freepik, licensed by http://creativecommons.org/licenses/by/3.0 Creative Commons BY 3.0
Back Cover	Author Photograph: Ryan McCullough
Layout/Design	Jennifer H. Kagan

Made in the USA
Monee, IL
18 April 2022